SANTA'S ON MEMORY LANE

ILLUSTRATED AND LARGE PRINT

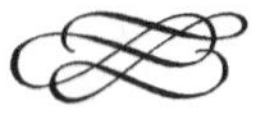

KRISTIN G HATCH

DELAINA J MILLER

ISBN-13: 978-1-942005-63-6 (Paperback edition)

ISBN-13: 978-1-942005-64-3 (Ebook edition)

www.contentxdesign.com

CONTENTS

A TOAST TO SANTA CLAUS

Whenever I find a man who don't
Believe in Santa Claus,
And spite of all firm protest won't
Yield up to logic's laws,
And see in things that lie about
The proof by no means dim,
I straight away cut that fellow out,
And don't believe in him.

The good old Saint is everywhere
Along life's busy way.
We find him in the very air
We breathe day after day—

Where courtesy and kindliness
And love are joined together,
To give to sorrow and distress
A touch of sunny weather.

We find him in the maiden's eyes
Beneath the mistletoe,
As sparkling as the starlit skies
All golden in their glow.
We find him in the pressure of
The hand of sympathy,
And where there's any thought
of love
He's mighty sure to be.

So, here's to good old Kindly-
heart!
The best bet of them all,
Who never fails to do his part
In life's high festival;
The worthy bearer of the crown,
With which we top the saint.
A bumper to his health, and down
With them that say he ain't!

CHRISTMAS DAY IN THE MORNING

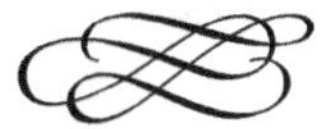

He woke suddenly and completely. It was four o'clock, the hour at which his father had always called him to get up and help with the milking. Strange how the habits of his youth clung to him still! Fifty years ago, and his father had been dead for thirty years, and yet he woke at four o'clock in the morning. He had trained himself to turn over and go to sleep, but this morning, because it was Christmas, he did not try to sleep.

Yet what was the magic of Christmas now? His childhood and youth were long past, and his own children had grown up and gone. Some of them lived only a few miles away but they had their own families, and though they would come in as usual toward the end of the day, they had explained with infinite gentleness that they wanted their children to build Christmas memories about their houses, not his. He was left alone with his wife.

Yesterday she had said, "It isn't worthwhile, perhaps—"

And he had said, "Oh, yes, Alice, even if there are only the two of us, let's have a Christmas of our own."

Then she had said, "Let's not trim the tree until tomorrow, Robert—just so it's ready when the children come. I'm tired."

He had agreed, and the tree was still out in the back entry.

Why did he feel so awake tonight? It was, after all, a still night, a clear and starry night. There was no moon, of course, but the stars were extraordinary! Now that he thought of it, the stars always seemed large and clear before the dawn of Christmas Day.

There was one star now that was certainly larger and brighter than any of the others. He could even imagine it moving, as it had seemed to move one night long ago.

He slipped back in time, as he did so easily nowadays. He was fifteen years old and still on his father's farm. He loved his father. He had not known it until one day, a few days before Christmas, when he had overheard what his father was saying to his mother.

"Mary, I hate to call Rob in the morning. He's growing so fast and he needs his sleep. If you could see how he sleeps when I go in to wake him up! I wish I could manage alone."

"Well, you can't, Adam." His mother's voice

was brisk. "Besides, he isn't a child anymore. It's time he took his turn."

"Yes," his father said slowly. "But I really don't want to wake him."

When he heard these words, something in him woke—his father loved him! He had never thought of it before, taking for granted the tie of their blood. Neither his father nor his mother talked about loving their children—they had no time for such things. There was always so much to do on a farm.

Now that he knew his father loved him, there would be no more wasting time in the mornings and having to be called again. He got up after that, stumbling blind with sleep, and pulled on his clothes, his eyes tight shut, but he got up.

And then on the night before Christmas, that year when he was fifteen, he lay for a few minutes thinking about the next day. They were poor, and most of the excitement was in the turkey they had raised themselves, and in the mince pies his mother made. His sisters sewed presents and his mother and father always bought something he needed, not only a warm jacket, maybe, but something more, such as a book. And he saved and bought them each something, too.

He wished, that Christmas he was fifteen, he had a better present for his father. As usual he had gone to the ten-cent store and bought a tie. It had seemed nice enough until he lay thinking the night before Christmas, and then he wished that he had heard his father and mother talking in time for him to save for something better.

He lay on his side, his head supported by his elbows, and looked out of his attic window. The starts were bright, much brighter than he ever remembered seeing them, and one star in particular was so bright that he wondered if it were really the Star of Bethlehem.

"Dad," he had once asked when he was a little boy, "what is a stable?"

"It's just a barn," his father had replied, "like ours."

Then Jesus Christ had been born in a barn and to a barn the shepherds and the wise men had come, bringing their Christmas gifts!

The thought struck him like a silver dagger. He could also give his father a special gift, out there in the barn! He could get up early, earlier than four o'clock, and he could go into the barn and do all the milking. He'd do it alone, milk and clean up, and then when his father went in to start the milking, he'd see it all done. And he would know who had done it.

He must have woken twenty times, scratching a match each time to look at his old watch—midnight, and half past one, and then two o'clock.

At a quarter to three he got up and put on his clothes. He crept downstairs, careful of the creaky boards, and let himself out. The big star hung lower over the barn roof, a reddish gold. The cows looked at him, sleepy and surprised. It was early for them, too.

"So, Boss," he whispered. They accepted him placidly and he fetched some hay for each cow and then got the milking pail and the big milk cans.

He had never milked all alone before, but it seemed almost easy. He kept thinking about his father's surprise. His father would come in and call him, saying that he would start while Rob was getting dressed. He'd go to the barn, open the door, and then he'd go to get the two big empty milk cans. But they wouldn't be waiting or empty; they'd be standing in the milk-house, filled with milk.

"What in the world?" he could hear his father exclaiming.

He smiled and milked steadily, two strong streams rushing into the bucket, bubbly and warm. The cows were still surprised but yielding. For once they were behaving well, as though they knew it was Christmas.

The task went more easily than he had ever known it to before. Milking for once was not a chore. It was something else, a gift to his father that loved him. He finished, the two milk cans were full, and he covered them and closed the milk-house door carefully, making sure the latch was closed. He put the stool in its place by the door and hung up the clean milk pail. Then he went out of the barn and locked the door behind him.

Back in his room he had only a minute to pull off his clothes in the darkness and jump into bed, before he heard his father.

"Rob!" his father called. "We have to get up, Son, even if it is Christmas."

"OK," he said sleepily.

"I'll go ahead," his father said. "I'll get things started."

The door closed and he lay still, laughing to himself. In just a few minutes his father would know. His dancing heart was ready to jump from his body.

The minutes were endless—ten, fifteen, he did not know how many—and then he heard his father's footsteps again. The door opened and he lay still.

"Rob!"

"Yes, Dad—"

"You son of a gun.. ." His father was laughing, an odd, sobbing sort of laugh.

"Thought you'd fool me, did you?" His father was standing beside his bed, feeling for him, pulling away the blanket.

"It's for Christmas, Dad!"

He found his father and clutched him in a great hug. He felt his father's arms go around him. It was dark and they could not see each other's faces.

"Son, I thank you. Nobody ever did a nicer thing—"

"Oh, Dad, I want you to know—I do want to be good!" The words broke from him of their own will. He did not know what to say. His heart was bursting with love.

"Well, I reckon I can go back to bed and sleep," his father said after a moment. "No, no—the little ones are waking up. Come to think of it, Son, I've never seen you children when you first saw the Christmas tree. I was always in the barn. Come on!"

Rob got up and pulled on his clothes again and they went down to the Christmas tree, and soon the sun was creeping up to where the star had been. Oh, what a Christmas, and how his heart had nearly burst again with shyness and pride as his father told his mother and made the younger children listen about how he, Rob, had gotten up all by himself.

"The best Christmas gift I ever had, and I'll remember it, Son, every year on Christmas morning, so long as I live."

They had both remembered it, and now that his father was dead he remembered it alone: that special Christmas dawn when, alone with the cows in the barn, he had made his first gift of true love.

Outside the window now the great star slowly sank. He got up out of the bed, put on his slippers and bathrobe, and went softly upstairs to the attic to find the box of Christmas tree decorations. He took them downstairs into the living room. Then he brought in the tree. It was a little one—they had not had a big tree since the children went away—but he set it in the holder and then on the long table under the window. Then carefully he began to trim it.

It was dawn very soon, the time passing as quickly as it had that morning long ago in the barn. He went to his library and fetched the little box that contained his special gift to his wife, a star of diamonds, not large but dainty in design. He had written the card for it the day before. He tied the gift on the tree and then stood back. It was pretty, very pretty, and she would be surprised.

However, he was not satisfied. He wanted to tell her—to tell her how much he loved her. It had been a long time since he had really told her, although he loved her in a very special way, much more than when they were young.

He had been fortunate that she had loved him—and how fortunate that he had been able to love.

Ah, that was the true joy of life, the ability to love! He was quite sure that some people were genuinely unable to love anyone, but love was alive in him, it still was.

It occurred to him suddenly that it was alive because long ago it had been born in him when he knew his father loved him. That was it: love alone could awaken love.

And he could give the gift again and again. This morning, this wonderful Christmas morning, he would give it to his beloved wife. He could write it down in a letter for her to read and keep forever. He went to his desk and began his love letter to his wife: "My dearest love.. ."

When it was finished, he sealed it and tied it on the tree where she would see it the first thing when she came into the room. She would read it, surprised, and then moved, and realize how very much he loved her.

He put out the light and went tiptoeing up the stairs. The star in the sky was gone, and the first rays of the sun were gleaming in the sky. Such a happy, happy Christmas.

A VISIT FROM ST. NICHOLAS

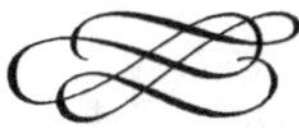

'Twas the night before Christmas
when all through the house
Not a creature was stirring, not
even a mouse;
The stockings were hung by the
chimney with care
In hopes that St. Nicholas soon
would be there.

The children were nestled all snug
in their beds,
While visions of sugarplums
danced in their heads;

And mamma in her kerchief, and I
in my cap,
Had just settled our brains for a
long winter's nap.

When out on the lawn there arose
such a clatter,
I sprang from the bed to see, what
was the matter.
Away to the window I flew like a
flash,
Tore open the shutters and threw
up the sash.

The moon on the breast of the
new-fallen snow
Gave the luster of mid-day to
objects below,
When, what to my wondering eyes
should appear,
But a miniature sleigh, and eight
tiny reindeer.

With a little old driver, so lively
and quick,

I knew in a moment it must be St.
Nick.
More rapid than eagles his
coursers they came,
And he whistled, and shouted, and
called them by name:

"Now, Dasher! Now, Dancer!
Now, Prancer and Vixen!
On, Comet! On, Cupid!
On, Donner and Blitzen!
To the top of the porch! To the top
of the wall!
Now dash away! Dash away! Dash
away all!"

As dry leaves that before the wild
hurricane fly,

When they meet with an obstacle,
mount to the sky;
So up to the house-top the coursers
they flew,
With the sleigh full of toys, and St.
Nicholas too.

And then, in a twinkling, I heard on
the roof
The prancing and pawing of each
little hoof.
As I drew in my head, and was
turning around,
Down the chimney St. Nicholas
came with a bound.

He was dressed all in fur, from his
head to his foot,
And his clothes were all tarnished
with ashes and soot;
A bundle of toys he had flung on
his back,
And he looked like a peddler just
opening his pack.

His eyes—how they twinkled! His
dimples how merry!
His cheeks were like roses, his nose
like a cherry!
His droll little mouth was drawn up
like a bow,
And the beard of his chin was as
white as the snow.

The stump of a pipe he held tight in
his teeth,
And the smoke, it encircled his
head like a wreath;
He had a broad face and a little
round belly,
That shook when he laughed, like a
bowlful of jelly.

He was chubby and plump, a right
jolly old elf,

And I laughed when I saw him, in
spite of myself;
A wink of his eye and a twist of his
head,
Soon gave me to know I had
nothing to dread.

He spoke not a word, but went
straight to his work,
And filled all the stockings; then
turned with a jerk,
And laying his finger aside of his
nose,
And giving a nod, up the chimney
he rose.

He sprang to his sleigh, to his team
gave a whistle,
And away they all flew like the
down of a thistle.
But I heard him exclaim, as he
drove out of sight,
"Happy Christmas to all, and to all
a good night!"

SANTA CLAUS AND LITTLE BILLY

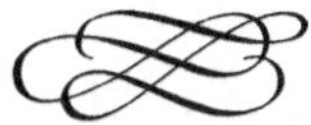

He was only a little bit of a chap, and so, when for the first time in his life he came into close contact with the endless current of human things, it was as hard for him to "stay put" as when he was but a tiny bobber tossing about in the surging tides of the sea. His mother had left him there in the big toyshop, with instructions not to move until she came back, while she went off to do some mysterious errand.

She thought, no doubt, that with so many beautiful things on every side to delight his eye and hold his attention, strict obedience to her commands would not be hard. But, alas, the good lady reckoned not upon the magnetic power of attraction of all those lovely objects in detail. She saw them only as a mass of wonders, which, in all probability, would so dazzle his vision as to leave him incapable of movement; but Little Billy was not so indifferent as all that.

When a phonograph at the other end of the shop began to rattle off pleasant tunes and funny jokes, in spite of the instructions he had received, off he scurried as fast as his little legs would carry him to investigate.

After that, forgetful of everything else, he found himself caught in the constantly moving stream of Christmas shoppers. He was swept along in the resistless current until he found himself, at last, out upon the street—alone, free, and independent.

It was great fun, at first. By and by, however, the afternoon waned. The sun, as if anxious to hurry along the dawn of Christmas Day, sank early to bed. The electric lights along the darkening highway began to pop out here and there, like so many merry stars come down to earth to celebrate the gladdest time of all the year. Little Billy began to grow tired. He thought of his mama and tried to find the shop where he had promised to remain quiet until her return. Up and down the street he wandered until his little legs grew weary; but there was no sign of the shop, nor of the beloved face he was seeking.

Once again, and yet once again after that, did the little fellow traverse that crowded highway, his tears getting harder and harder to keep back, and then—joy of joys—whom should he see walking slowly along the sidewalk but Santa Claus himself!

The saint was strangely decorated with two odd-looking boards, with big red letters on them, hung over his back and chest. Yet there was still that same kind, gray-bearded face, the red cloak with the fur trimmings, and the same dear old cap —that the children's friend had always worn in the pictures of him that Little Billy had seen.

With a glad cry of happiness, Little Billy ran to meet the old fellow, and put his hand gently into that of the saint. He thought it very strange that Santa Claus's hand should be so red and cold and rough, and so chapped. But he was not in any mood to be critical. He had been face-to-face with a very disagreeable situation. Then, when things had seemed darkest to him, everything had come right again. He was too glad to take more than passing notice of anything strange and odd.

Santa Claus, of course, would recognize him at once, and would know just how to take him back to his mama at home—wherever that might be. Little Billy had never thought to inquire just where home was. All he knew was that it was a big gray stone house on a long street somewhere, with a tall iron railing in front of it, not far from the park.

"Howdidoo, Mr. Santa Claus?" said Little Billy, as the other's hand unconsciously tightened over his own.

"Why, howdidoo, kiddie?" replied the old fellow, glancing down at his new-found friend, with surprise gleaming from his deep-set eyes. "Where did you drop from?"

"Oh, I'm out," said Little Billy bravely. "My mama left me a little while ago while she went off about something, and I guess I got losted."

"Very likely," returned the old saint with a smile. "Little two-by-four fellows are apt to get losted when they start in on their own hook, specially days like these, with such crowds hustlin' around."

"But it's all right now," suggested Little Billy hopefully. "I'm found again, ain't I?"

"Oh, yes, indeedy, you're found all right, kiddie," Santa Claus agreed.

"And pretty soon you'll take me home again, won't you?" said the child.

"Surest thing you know!" answered Santa Claus, looking down upon the bright but tired little face with a comforting smile. "What might your address be?"

"My what?" asked Little Billy.

"Your address," repeated Santa Claus. "Where do you live?"

The answer was a ringing peal of childish laughter. "As if you didn't know that!" cried Little Billy, giggling.

"Ha, ha!" laughed Santa Claus. "Can't fool you, can I? It would be funny if, after keeping an eye on you all these years since you was a baby, I didn't know where you lived, eh?"

"Awful funny," agreed Little Billy. "But tell me, Mr. Santa Claus, what sort of a boy do you think I have been?" he added with a shade of anxiety in his voice.

"Pretty good—pretty good," Santa Claus answered, turning in his steps, and walking back again along the path he had just traveled—which Little Billy thought was rather a strange thing to do. "You've got more good marks than bad ones—a good many more—a hundred and fifty times as many, kiddie. Fact is, you're all right—'way up among the good boys; though once or twice last summer, you know—"

"Yes, I know," said Little Billy meekly, "but I didn't mean to be naughty."

"That's just what I said to the bookkeeper," said Santa Claus, "and so we gave you a half mark that doesn't count either way, for or against you."

"Thank you, sir," said Little Billy, much comforted.

"Don't mention it; you are very welcome, kiddie," said Santa Claus, giving the youngster's hand a gentle squeeze.

"Why do you call me 'kiddie' when you know my name is Little Billy?" asked the boy.

"Oh, that's what I call all good boys," explained Santa Claus. "You see, we divide them up into two kinds—the good boys and the naughty boys—and the good boys we call kiddies, and the naughty boys we call cads, and there you are."

Just then Little Billy noticed for the first time the square boards that Santa Claus was wearing.

"What are you wearing those boards for, Mr. Santa Claus?" he asked.

If the lad had looked closely enough, he would have seen a very unhappy look come into the old man's face; but there was nothing of it in his answer.

"Oh, those are my new-fangled back-and-chest protectors, my lad," he replied. "Sometimes we have bitter winds blowing at Christmas, and I have to be ready for them. It wouldn't do for Santa Claus to come down with the sneezes at Christmas time, you know—no, sirree! This board in front keeps the wind off my chest, and the one behind keeps me from getting rheumatism in my back. They are a great protection against the weather."

"I'll have to tell my papa about them," said Little Billy, much impressed by the simplicity of this arrangement. "We have a glass board on the front of our ortymobile to keep the wind off Henry—he's our shuffer—but papa wears a fur coat, and sometimes he says the wind goes right through that. He'll be glad to know about these boards."

"I shouldn't wonder," smiled Santa Claus. "They aren't very becoming, but they are mighty useful. You might save up your pennies and give your papa a pair like 'em for his next Christmas." Santa Claus laughed as he spoke; but there was a catch in his voice, which Little Billy was too young to notice.

"You've got letters printed there," said the boy, peering around in front of his companion at the lettering on the board. "What do they spell? You know I haven't learned to read yet."

"And why should you know how to read at your age?" said Santa Claus. "You're not more than—"

"Five last month," said Little Billy proudly. It was such a great age!

"My, as old as that?" cried Santa Claus. "Well, you are growing fast! Why, it doesn't seem more than yesterday that you was a pink-cheeked baby, and here you are big enough to be out alone! That's more than my little boy is able to do."

Santa Claus shivered slightly, and Little Billy was surprised to see a tear glistening in his eye.

"Why, have you got a little boy?" he asked.

"Yes, Little Billy," said the saint. "A poor white-faced little chap, about a year older than you, who—well, never mind, kiddie—he's a kiddie, too—let's talk about something else, or I'll have icicles in my eyes."

"You didn't tell me what those letters on the boards spell," said Little Billy.

Merry Christmas!

"'Merry Christmas to Everybody!'" said Santa Claus. "I have the words printed there so that everybody can see them; and if I miss wishing anybody a merry Christmas, they will know I meant it just the same."

"You're awful kind, aren't you?" said Little Billy, squeezing his friend's hand affectionately. "It must make you very happy to be able to be so kind to everybody!"

Santa Claus made no reply to this remark, beyond giving a very deep sigh, which Little Billy chose to believe was evidence of a great inward content. They walked on now in silence, for Little Billy was beginning to feel almost too tired to talk, and Santa Claus seemed to be thinking of something else. Finally, however, the little fellow spoke.

"I guess I'd like to go home now, Mr. Santa Claus," he said. "I'm tired, and I'm afraid my mama will be wondering where I've gone to."

"That's so, my little man," said Santa Claus, stopping short in his walk up and down the block. "Your mother will be worried, for a fact; and your father, too—I know how I'd feel if my little boy got losted and hadn't come home at dinner-time. I don't believe you know where you live, though—now, honest! Come! 'Fess up, Billy, you don't know where you live, do you?"

"Why, yes, I do," said Little Billy. "It's in the big gray stone house with the iron fence in front of it, near the park."

"Oh, that's easy enough!" laughed Santa Claus nervously. "Anybody could say he lived in a gray stone house with a fence around it, near the park; but you don't know what street it's on, nor the number, either. I'll bet fourteen wooden giraffes against a monkey-on-a-stick!"

"No, I don't," said Little Billy frankly; "but I know the number of our ortymobile. It's 'N. Y.'"

"Fine!" laughed Santa Claus. "If you really were lost, it would be a great help to know that; but not being lost, as you ain't, why, of course, we can get along without it. It's odd you don't know your last name, though."

"I do, too, know my last name!" blurted Little

Billy. "It's Billy. That's the last one they gave me, anyhow."

Santa Claus reflected for a moment, eying the child anxiously. "I don't believe you even know your papa's name," he said.

"Yes, I do," said Little Billy indignantly. "His name is Mr. Harrison."

"Well, you are a smart little chap," cried Santa Claus gleefully. "You got it right the very first time, didn't you? I really didn't think you knew. But I don't believe you know where your papa keeps his bake shop, where he makes all those nice cakes and cookies you eat."

Billy began to laugh again. "You can't fool me, Mr. Santa Claus," he said. "I know my papa don't keep a bake shop just as well as you do. My papa owns a bank."

"Splendid! Made of tin, I suppose, with a nice little hole at the top to drop pennies into?" said Santa Claus.

"No, it ain't, either!" retorted Little Billy. "It's made of stone and has more than a million windows in it. I went down there with my mama to papa's office the other day, so I guess I ought to know."

"Well, I should say so," said Santa Claus. "Nobody better. By the way, Billy, what does your mama call your papa? 'Billy,' like you?" he added.

"Oh, no, indeed," returned Little Billy. "She calls him papa, except once in a while, when he's going away, and then she says, 'Good-bye, Tom. '

"Fine again!" said Santa Claus, blowing upon his fingers, for now that the sun had completely disappeared over in the west, it was getting very cold. "Thomas Harrison, banker," he muttered to himself. "What with the telephone-book and the city directory, I guess we can find our way home with Little Billy."

"Do you think we can go now, Mr. Santa Claus?" asked Little Billy, for the cold was beginning to cut through his little coat, and the sandman had started to scatter the sleepy-seeds all around.

"Yes, sirree!" returned Santa Claus promptly. "Right away off now instantly at once! I'm afraid I can't get my reindeer here in time to take us up to the house, but we can go in the cars—hum! I don't know whether we can or not, come to think of it. Ah, do you happen to have ten cents in your pocket?" Santa added with an embarrassed air. "You see, I've left my pocketbook in the sleigh with my toy-pack; and, besides, mine is only toy-money, and they won't take that on the cars."

"I got twenty-fi' cents," said Little Billy proudly, as he dug his way down into his pocket and brought the shining silver piece to light. "You can have it, if you want it."

"Thank you," said Santa Claus, taking the offered coin. "We'll start home right away; only come in here first, while I telephone to Santaville, telling the folks where I am."

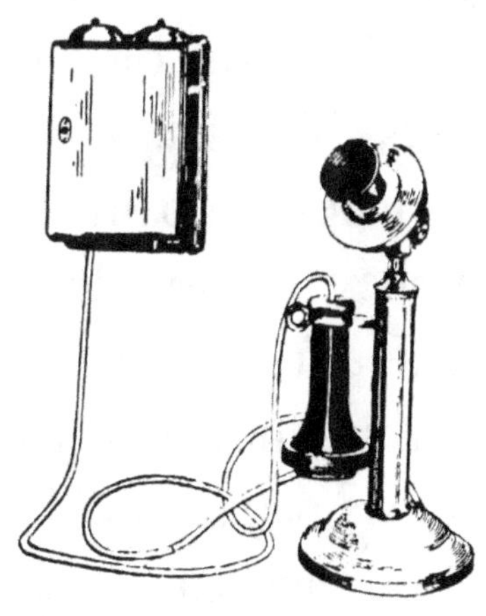

He led the little fellow into a public telephone station, where he eagerly scanned the names in the book. At last it was found—"Thomas Harrison, seven-six-five-four Plaza." And then, in the seclusion of the telephone-booth, Santa Claus sent the gladdest of all Christmas messages over the wire to two distracted parents:

"I have found your boy wandering in the street. He is safe, and I will bring him home right away."

Fifteen minutes later, there might have been seen the strange spectacle of a foot-sore Santa Claus leading a sleepy little boy up Fifth Avenue to a cross-street, which shall be nameless. The boy vainly endeavored to persuade his companion to "come in and meet mama."

"No, Billy," the old man replied sadly, "I must hurry back. You see, kiddie, this is my busy day. Besides, I never go into a house except through the chimney. I wouldn't know how to behave, going in at a front door."

But it was not to be as Santa Claus willed, for Little Billy's papa, and his mama, and his brothers and sisters, and the butler and the housemaids, and two or three policemen, were waiting at the front door when they arrived.

"Aha!" said one of the police, seizing Santa Claus roughly by the arm. "We've landed you, all right! Where have you been with this boy?"

"You let him alone!" cried Little Billy, with more courage than he had ever expected to show in the presence of a policeman. "He's a friend of mine."

"That's right, officer," said Little Billy's father, "let him alone—I haven't entered any complaint against this man."

"But you want to look out for these fellers, Mr. Harrison," returned the officer. "First thing you know they'll be makin' a trade of this sort of thing."

"I'm no grafter!" retorted Santa Claus indignantly. "I found the little chap wandering along the street, and, as soon as I was able to locate where he lived, I brought him home. That's all there is to it."

"He knew where I lived all along," laughed Little Billy, "only he pretended he didn't, just to see if I knew."

"You see, sir," said the officer, "it won't do him any harm to let him cool his heels."

"It is far better that he should warm them, officer," said Mr. Harrison kindly. "And he can do that here. Come in, my man," he added, turning to Santa Claus with a grateful smile. "Just for a minute anyhow. Mrs. Harrison will wish to thank you for bringing our boy back to us. We have had a terrible afternoon."

"That's all right, sir," said Santa Claus modestly. "It wasn't anything, sir. I didn't really find him—it was him as found me, sir. He took me for the real thing, I guess."

Nevertheless, Santa Claus, led by Little Billy's persistent father, went into the house. Now that the boy could see him in the full glare of many electric lights, his furs did not seem the most gorgeous things in the world. When the flapping front of his red jacket flew open, the child was surprised to see how ragged was the thin gray coat it covered; and as for the good old saint's comfortable stomach—strange to say, it was not!

"I—I wish you all a merry Christmas," faltered Santa Claus, "but I really must be going, sir—"

"Nonsense!" cried Mr. Harrison. "Not until you have got rid of this chill, and—"

"I can't stay, sir," said Santa. "I'll lose my job if I do."

"Well, what if you do? I'll give you a better one," said the banker.

"I can't—I can't!" faltered the man. "I—I—I've got a Little Billy of my own at home waitin' for me, sir. If I hadn't," he added fiercely, "do you suppose I'd be doin' this?" He pointed at the painted boards and shuddered. "It's him as has kept me from—from the river!" he muttered hoarsely; and then this dispenser of happiness to so many millions of people all the world over sank into a chair, and, covering his face with his hands, wept like a child.

"I guess Santa Claus is tired, papa," said Little Billy, snuggling up closely to the old fellow and taking hold of his hand sympathetically. "He's been walkin' a lot to-day."

"Yes, my son," said Mr. Harrison gravely. "These are very busy times for Santa Claus, and I guess that, as he still has a hard night ahead of him, James had better ring up Henry and tell him to bring the car around right away, so that we may take him back—to his little boy. We'll have to lend him a fur coat to keep the wind off, too, for it is a bitter night."

"Oh," said Little Billy, "I haven't told you about these boards he wears. He has 'em to keep the wind off, and they're fine, papa!" Little Billy pointed to the two sign boards which Santa Claus had leaned against the wall. "He says he uses 'em on cold nights," the lad went on. "They have writing on 'em, too. Do you know what it says?"

"Yes," said Mr. Harrison, glancing at the boards. "It says 'If You Want a Good Christmas Dinner for a Quarter, Go to Smithers's Café.'"

Little Billy roared with laughter.

"Papa's trying to fool me, just as you did when you pretended not to know where I lived, Santa Claus," he said, looking up into the old fellow's face, his own expression brimming over with mirth. "You mustn't think he can't read, though," the lad added hastily. "He's only joking."

"Oh, no, indeed, I shouldn't have thought that," replied Santa Claus, smiling through his tears.

"I've been joking, have I?" said Little Billy's papa. "Well, then, Mr. Billiam, suppose you inform me what it says on those boards."

"'Merry Christmas to Everybody,'" said Little Billy proudly. "I couldn't read it myself, but he told me what it said. He has it printed there so that if he misses saying it to anybody, they'll know he means it just the same."

"By Jove, Mr. Santa Claus," cried Little Billy's papa, grasping the old man warmly by the hand, "I owe you ten million apologies! I haven't believed in you for many a long year; but now, sir, I take it all back. You do exist, and, by the great horn spoon, you are the real thing!"

Little Billy had the satisfaction of acting as host to Santa Claus at a good, luscious dinner, which Santa Claus must have enjoyed very much, because, when explaining why he was so hungry, it came out that the poor old chap had been so busy all day that he had not had time to get any lunch—no, not even one of those good dinners at Smithers's café, to which Little Billy's father had jokingly referred. And after dinner Henry came with the automobile and, bidding everybody good night, Santa Claus and Little Billy's papa went out of the house together.

Christmas morning dawned, and Little Billy awoke from wonderful dreams of rich gifts, and of extraordinary adventures with his new-found friend, to find the reality quite as splendid as the dream things.

Later, what was his delight when a small boy, not much older than himself—a pale, thin, but playful little fellow—arrived at the house to spend the day with him, bringing with him a letter from Santa Claus himself! This was what the letter said:

> Dear Little Billy:—You must not tell anybody except your papa and your mama, but the little boy who brings you this letter is my little boy, and I am going to let you have him for a playfellow for Christmas Day. Treat him kindly for his papa's sake, and if you think his papa is worth loving, tell him so. Do not forget me, Little Billy. I shall see you often in the future, but I doubt if you will see me. I am not going to return to Twenty-Third Street again but shall continue my work in the Land of Yule, in the Palace of Good-Will, whose beautiful windows look out upon the homes of all good children.
>
> Good-bye, Little Billy, and the happiest of happy Christmases to you and all of yours.
>
> Affectionately,
> Santa Claus.

When Little Billy's mama read this to him that

Christmas morning, a stray little tear ran down her cheek and fell upon Little Billy's hand.

"Why, what are you crying for, mama?" he asked.

"With happiness, my dear little son," his mother answered. "I was afraid yesterday that I might have lost my little boy forever, but now— "

"You have an extra one thrown in for Christmas, haven't you?" said Little Billy, taking his new playmate by the hand. The visitor smiled back at him with a smile so sweet that anybody might have guessed that he was the son of Santa Claus.

As for the latter, Little Billy has not seen him again; but down at his father's bank there is a new messenger, named John, who has a voice so like Santa Claus's voice that whenever Little Billy goes down there in the motor to ride home at night with his papa, he runs into the bank and has a long talk with him, just for the pleasure of pretending that it is Santa Claus he is talking to. Indeed, the voice is so like that once a sudden and strange idea flashed across Little Billy's mind.

"Have you ever been on Twenty-Third Street, John?" he asked.

"Twenty-Third Street?" replied the messenger, scratching his head as if very much puzzled. "What's that?"

"Why, it's a street," said Little Billy rather vaguely.

"Well, to tell you the truth, Billy," said John, "I've heard tell of Twenty-Third Street, and they say it is a very beautiful and interesting spot. But, you know, I don't get much chance to travel. I've been too busy all my life to go abroad."

"Abroad!" roared Little Billy, grinning at John's utterly absurd mistake. "Why, Twenty-Third Street ain't abroad! It's up-town—near—oh, near—Twenty-Second Street."

"Really?" returned John, evidently tremendously surprised. "Well, well, well! Who'd have thought that? Well, if that's the case, some time when I get a week off, I'll have to go and spend my vacation there!"

From which Little Billy concluded that his suspicion that John might be Santa Claus in disguise, was entirely without foundation in fact.

SANTA CLAUS

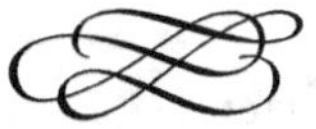

A voice from out of the northern
sky:
"On the wings of the limitless
winds I fly.
Swifter than thought, over
mountain and vale,
City and moorland, desert, and
dale!
From the north to the south, from
the east to the west
I hasten regardless of slumber or
rest;

O, nothing you dream of can fly
as fast
As I on the wings of the windy
blast!

"The wondering stars look out
to see
Who he that flieth so fast may be,
And their bright eyes follow my
earthward track
By the gleam of the jewels I bear in
my pack.
For I have treasures for high and
for low:
Rubies that burn like the sunset
glow;
Diamond rays for the crowned
queen;
For the princess pearls with their
silver sheen.

"I enter the castle with noiseless
feet—
The air is silent and soft and sweet;
And I lavish my beautiful tokens

there—
Fairings to make the fair more
fair!
I enter the cottage of want
and woe—
The candle is dim and the fire
burns low;
But the sleepers smile in a happy
dream
As I scatter my gifts by the moon's
pale beam.

"There's never a home so low, no
doubt.
But I in my flight can find it out;
Not a hut so hidden but I can see
The shadow cast by the lone
rooftree!
There's never a home so proud
and high
That I am constrained to pass it by,
Nor a heart so happy it may not be
Happier still when blessed by me!

"What is my name? Ah, who can

tell,
Though in every land 'tis a magic spell?
Men call me that, and they call me this;
Yet the different names are the same, I wish!
Gift-bearer to all the world am I,
Joy-giver, light-bringer, where'er I fly;
But the name I bear in the courts above,
My truest and holiest name, is —LOVE!"

ACKNOWLEDGMENTS

A glimpse at the authors and their original works (before we got our hands on their stories to up-cycle and polish the breath of their words)

"A Toast to Santa Claus" (1912) & "Santa Claus and Little Billy" (1912) by John Kendrick Bangs were both found in *A Little Book of Christmas*.

Bangs was born in Yonkers, New York, on May 27, 1862. He was a satirical writer and a jokester. He entertained allied troops in France during World War I.

“Christmas Day in the Morning” by Pearl S. Buck (1955)

Pearl Sydenstricker Buck was born in Hillsboro, West Virginia on June 26, 1892. She was the daughter of missionaries and spent most of her life until 1934 in China. She was the first American woman to win the Nobel Prize for Literature in 1938.

“A Visit from St. Nicholas” attributed to Clement Clarke Moore (1837)

Moore was born in New York City, New York on July 15, 1779. Moore was credited with writing the famous poems on a snowy winter’s day during a shopping trip on a sleigh. His St. Nick was inspired by local Dutch handymen, among other influences.

“Santa Claus” (1897) by Julia C. R. Dorr was included in *Christmas Entertainments* by Alice Kellogg.

Born Julia Caroline Ripley Dorr in Charleston, South Carolina, on February 13, 1825. She is known most for her poetry and her ability to string words together that allow others to see what she saw.

OTHER UP-CYCLED & LARGE PRINT BOOKS

KRISTIN G HATCH & DELAINA J MILLER OF CONTENT X DESIGN

The Man Who Would be King

Peace River Joe

Holiday Cheer : This Makes Me Smile

This Makes Me Smile

* * *

Please check our website for our full selection of positive publications.

www.contentxdesign.com

www.ingramcontent.com/pod-product-compliance
Lightning Source LLC
Chambersburg PA
CBHW070453170726
48291CB00005B/1739